MW00463069

Europe meets USA
Europa trifft USA
Europe/États-Unis, mode d'emploi
Europa se encuentra con EE. UU.

A book by **Yang Liu**

My name has a meaning: "Across the sea and into the distance." Is that why I started looking at world maps and globes so early on, dreaming of the day I would cross one of those oceans? The most exotic place I could imagine in Beijing back then was the United States of America—the country that lies on the other side of the ocean I was named after. In the mid-1980s, we did move abroad, but not to the US—we moved to Germany, to the center of Europe. Moving to the US, however, never left my mind. After finishing my studies, I made it across the Atlantic and lived in the United States for quite a while. So much there honestly exceeded my expectations; some things surprised and shocked me. I realized how different many aspects of everyday life were there in comparison with Central Europe. Today, I live in Berlin again, and over time, the enthusiasm of constant comparison has transformed into sober contemplation and reflection. So, I began documenting my thoughts and observations over the last few decades and capturing my view of the differences between the US and Europe in pictures. I hope the resulting little book will help minimize the misunderstandings and prejudices that exist between these two places despite their historical kinship and contribute to a mutual understanding of people on both sides of the ocean.

– Yang Liu

Mein Name trägt die Bedeutung „Über das Meer und die Ferne gehen".
Habe ich deshalb so früh angefangen, Weltkarten und Globusse anzu-
schauen und mir die Zeit auszumalen, zu der ich einen der Ozeane über-
queren würde? Das Exotischste, was ich mir damals in Peking vorstellen
konnte, war das Land, von dem mich eben dieses namensgebende Meer
trennte, die USA. Wir zogen dann tatsächlich Mitte der 1980er-Jahre ins
Ausland, jedoch nicht dorthin, sondern nach Deutschland, in die Mitte
Europas. Der Umzug in die Vereinigten Staaten stand aber immer im
Raum. Nach dem Studium gelang mir der Schritt über den Atlantik,
und ich lebte längere Zeit in den USA. Vieles dort übertraf meine
Erwartungen regelrecht, manches überraschte und schockierte mich.
Dabei fiel mir auf, wie unterschiedlich zu Mitteleuropa sich der Alltag
in zahlreichen Punkten gestaltete. Heute lebe ich wieder in Berlin, und
im Laufe der Zeit wandelte sich der Enthusiasmus durch den stetigen
Vergleich in nüchterne Betrachtung und Reflektion. Also fing ich an,
meine Gedanken und Beobachtungen der letzten Jahrzehnte zu dokumen-
tieren und die Unterschiede zwischen den USA und Europa aus meiner
persönlichen Sicht bildlich festzuhalten. Ich hoffe, dass dieses daraus
hervorgegangene Büchlein hilft, die trotz der historischen Verwandt-
schaft vorhandenen Missverständnisse und Vorurteile zu minimieren,
und, dass es zum gegenseitigen Verstehen der Menschen auf beiden
Seiten des Ozeans beiträgt.

– Yang Liu

Mon nom a pour signification « aller au-delà de la mer et au loin ». Est-ce pour cela que j'ai commencé très tôt à observer les cartes du monde et les globes terrestres et à m'imaginer le moment où je traverserais l'un des océans ? Je ne pouvais alors rien me figurer de plus exotique, lorsque je vivais à Pékin, que les États-Unis, pays dont me séparait précisément la mer qu'on retrouve dans mon nom. Mais si nous sommes bien partis à l'étranger au milieu des années 80, ce fut en Allemagne, au cœur de l'Europe. Le déménagement aux États-Unis est cependant toujours resté dans l'air. C'est après mes études que j'ai enfin réussi à franchir l'Atlantique et à vivre un certain temps sur le sol américain. Beaucoup de ce que j'y ai vu a sincèrement dépassé toutes mes attentes, et certaines choses m'ont surprise et choquée. Je me suis alors rendue compte à quel point le quotidien différait de celui en Europe à bien des égards. Aujourd'hui, je vis de nouveau à Berlin et avec le temps, mon enthousiasme pour ces comparaisons permanentes s'est mué en simple réflexion. C'est ainsi que j'ai commencé à documenter mes pensées et mes observations des dernières décennies et à fixer en images les différences entre les États-Unis et l'Europe d'un point de vue personnel. J'espère que ce petit livre aidera à réduire les malentendus et les préjugés qui existent malgré les liens de parenté historiques entre ces deux pays, et qu'il contribuera à une meilleure compréhension réciproque des habitants de chaque côté de l'Atlantique.

– Yang Liu

Mi nombre significa «ir a la otra orilla del mar y a lo lejos». ¿Será por esto por lo que empecé tan pronto a mirar mapamundis y el globo terráqueo, soñando con el día en el que cruzaría uno de esos océanos? Cuando vivía en Pekín, el lugar más exótico que alcanzaba a imaginar era EE. UU., el país que está en la otra orilla del mar que encierra mi nombre. A mediados de la década de 1980, migramos, pero no a EE. UU. sino a Alemania, en el centro de Europa. Sin embargo, nunca abandoné la idea de ir a vivir a Estados Unidos. Cuando acabé los estudios, crucé por fin el Atlántico y viví mucho tiempo en EE. UU. Tuve experiencias que superaron con creces mis expectativas, y hubo cosas que me sorprendieron y me impactaron. Me llamó la atención lo distintos que eran muchos aspectos de la vida cotidiana en comparación con el centro de Europa. Hoy día vuelvo a vivir en Berlín y, con el tiempo, mi entusiasmo por la comparación constante se ha transformado en mera contemplación y reflexión. Así fue como empecé a documentar mis pensamientos y observaciones de las últimas décadas y a plasmar en ilustraciones mi visión de las diferencias entre EE. UU. y Europa. El resultado es este librito, que espero que ayude a contrarrestar los malentendidos y prejuicios que existen entre ambos lugares, pese a su vínculo histórico, y que contribuya a un entendimiento mutuo a ambos lados del charco.

– Yang Liu

normal
normal
normal

freundlich
amical
amable

sehr freundlich
très amical
muy amable

normal

friendly

very friendly

„Wie geht's?" · «Comment ça va ?» · «¿Cómo va?»

sehr gut
très bien
muy bien

gut
bien
bien

es geht
ça va
va

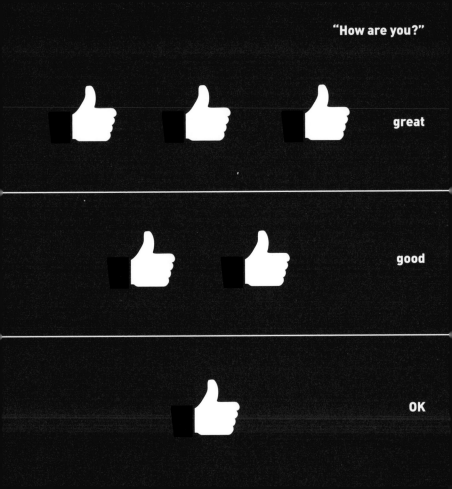

Languages

Perceived knowledge of the US · **Empfundenes Wissen über die USA**
Connaissance perçue des États-Unis · *Conocimiento percibido de EE. UU.*

Knowledge of the US · **Wissen über die USA** · Connaissance des États-Unis
Conocimiento de EE. UU.

Perceived knowledge of Europe · Empfundenes Wissen über Europa
Connaissance perçue de l'Europe · *Conocimiento percibido de Europa*

Knowledge of Europe · Wissen über Europa · Connaissance de l'Europe
Conocimiento de Europa

g ml l

SUN

Getränke · Boissons · *Bebidas*

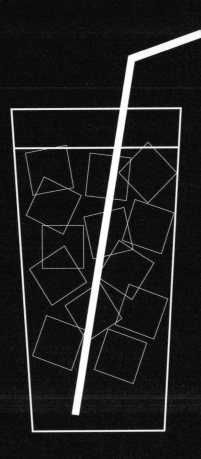

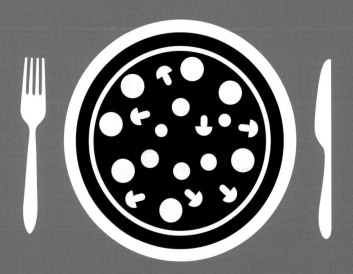

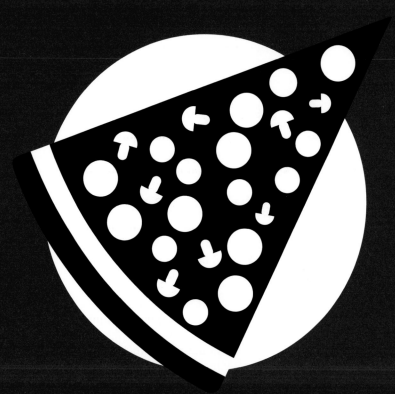

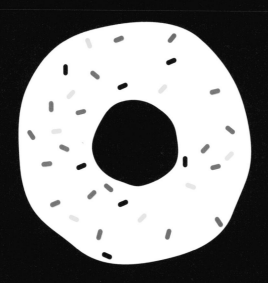

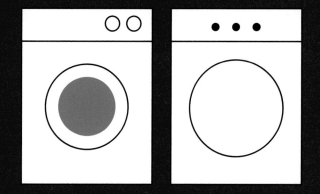

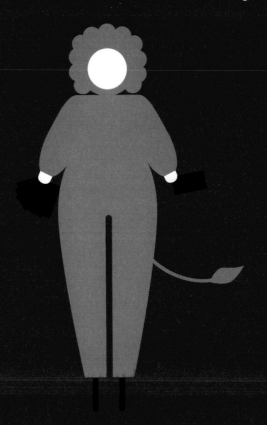

Straßenschilder
Panneaux de signalisation
Señales de tráfico

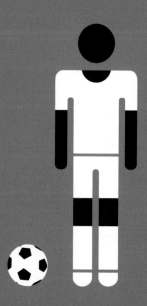

Publikum in der Oper · Public à l'opéra · *Público en la ópera*

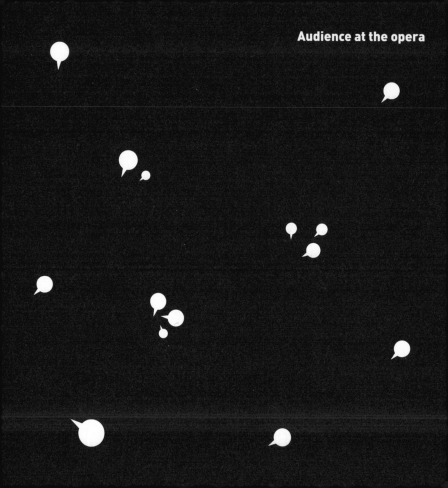

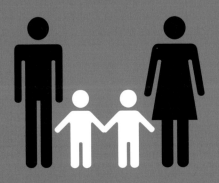

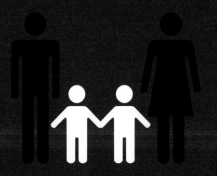

Durchschnittseuropäer · Europäischer Politiker
Européen moyen · Homme politique européen
Europeo medio · Político europeo

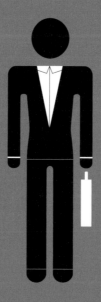

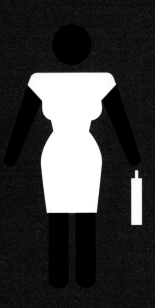

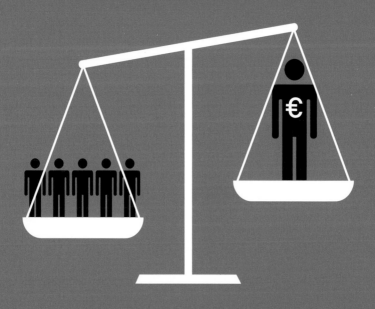

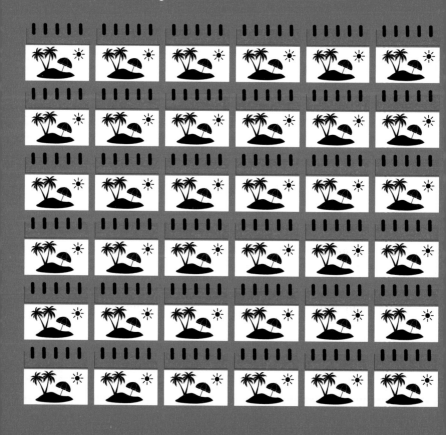

Urlaubsanspruch · Congés annuels · *Vacaciones anuales*

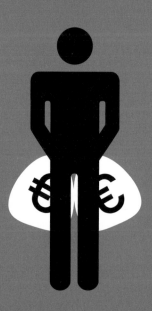

Europeans · Europäer · Européens · *Europeos*

Non-Europeans · Nicht-Europäer
Non-Européens · *No europeos*

US citizens · US-Amerikaner · Américains · *Estadounidenses*

Non-US citizens · Nicht-US-Amerikaner
Non-Américains · *No estadounidenses*

Migranten · Immigrants · *Migrantes*

10 Jahre später · 10 ans après · *10 años después*

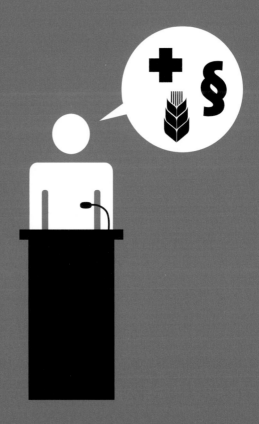

Held · Héros · *Héroe*

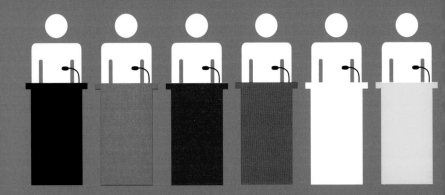

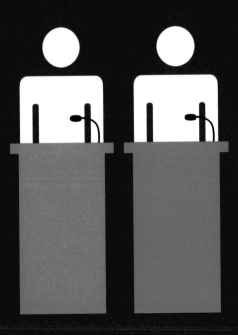

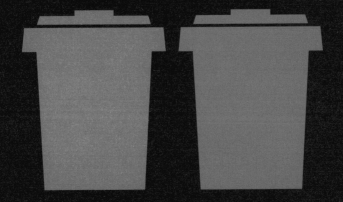

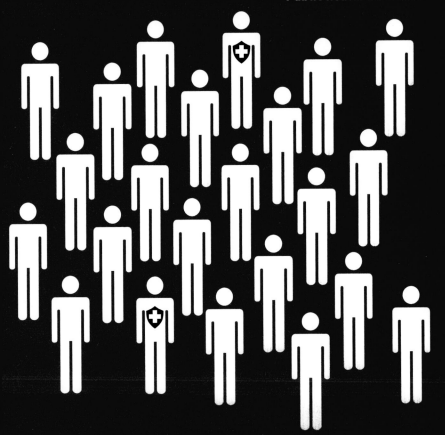

Public health insurance

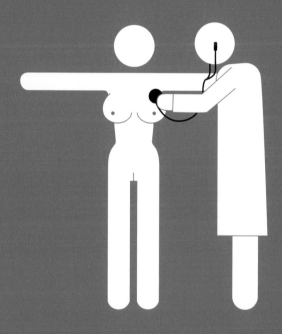

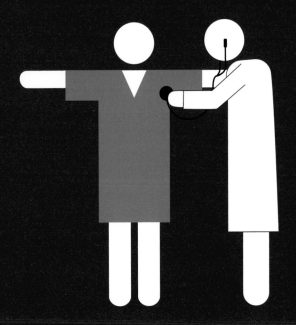

Romantik · Romance · *Romanticismo*

Ende von Liebesfilmen · Fin des films d'amour
Final de las películas románticas

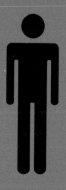

Yang Liu was born in 1976 in Beijing and moved to Germany at the age of 13. After studying at the University of Arts Berlin (UdK), she worked as a designer in Singapore, London, Berlin, and New York. In 2004 she founded her own design studio, which she continues to run today. In addition to holding workshops and lectures at international conferences, she has taught at numerous universities in Germany and abroad. In 2010 she was appointed a professor at the BTK University of Applied Sciences in Berlin. Her works have won numerous prizes in international competitions and can be found in museums and collections all over the world.

Yang Liu lives and works in Berlin.

Photo: Detlef Eden

EACH AND EVERY TASCHEN BOOK PLANTS A SEED!

TASCHEN is a carbon neutral publisher. Each year, we offset our annual carbon emissions with carbon credits at the Instituto Terra, a reforestation program in Minas Gerais, Brazil, founded by Lélia and Sebastião Salgado. To find out more about this ecological partnership, please check: www.taschen.com/zerocarbon.

Inspiration: unlimited.
Carbon footprint: zero.

To stay informed about TASCHEN and our upcoming titles, please subscribe to our free magazine at www.taschen.com/magazine, follow us on Instagram and Facebook, or e-mail your questions to contact@taschen.com.

Europe meets USA
A book by **Yang Liu**

Idea/Design © Yang Liu

© Copyright of all
artwork and text by
Yang Liu Design
Torstraße 185 · 10115 Berlin
www.yangliudesign.com

English translation: Hayley Haupt
French translation: Claire Debard
Spanish translation: Carme Franch
for Delivering iBooks

© 2022 TASCHEN GmbH
Hohenzollernring 53 · 50672 Cologne
www.taschen.com

ISBN 978-3-8365-9212-3

Printed in Slovakia